BUILT LIKE A BRICK OVEN

AND WHAT A REAR CHIMNEY!

WALT VINOSKI

Printed in the United States of America

First Printing: October 2013

Library of Congress Cataloging in Publication Data.
Walt Vinoski

Built Like a Brick Oven, and what a rear chimney.

Includes bibliographical references and index.
ISBN 13: 9781492831587
ISBN 10: 1492831581
Library of Congress Control Number: 2013919751
CreateSpace Independent Publishing Platform
North Charleston, South Carolina

ISBN (Alk. Paper)
1. Oven 2. Brick I. Vinoski, Walter II. Title

Publisher Information

DEDICATION

I dedicate this book to Roxanne, a woman who has stood beside me for decades, my partner. And to my dad, as he would be having the time of his life if he were still here with us, but until we meet again, I am sure I will have an occasional burnt offering for him to enjoy.

TABLE OF CONTENTS

ACKNOWLEDGMENTS

I thank my beautiful wife, Roxanne, for granting me time and encouraging me to write this book to help others as well as build the oven, and my wonderful children, Walter, Isabella, and Luke, for putting up with all my bantering about what we would be cooking after the oven was completed and a poem for them to remember: (*Mary had a little lamb, her father shot it dead. She still takes her lamb to school between two hunks of bread*). A thank you to my bricklayer Doug Walt and his helpers who did most of the work so all our friends and family can enjoy the fruits of our labor.

FORWARD

I study things endlessly (or at least it seems), and I try to understand the nuances and attributes of designs and features of things I build or have built, now that I seem to have less time. The basic idea of a bread oven is very appealing, and what is very old has become new again, but what I struggled with for years is what type of design should I use? What should it look like, how will I use it, and what modern day technologies add or subtract from its beauty and usefulness? What you are probably doing now, I have done—searched the Internet looking at dozens of designs, styles, and ideas and collecting the parts and pieces of those that you like. Combine features and move forward. You will see in the guide a way to build an oven; your oven will not look like this, and I encourage you to tailor your own design to your own needs and architecture. What you cannot figure out can be solved by someone else, maybe your local bricklayer. A portion of my efforts here are made to encourage you to keep moving forward and building your own brick oven.

PROLOGUE

My ancestors all had brick ovens; it's not just Polish, French, Italian, or European. It was a convenience, and these ovens were often located at the town square if fuel was scarce. Old World European high-heat cooking ovens were the first true fast-food eateries, searing meats and vegetables in minutes. And yes, with a live wood or coal fire, you can make superb pizza in two minutes and cook steaks, shoulders, roasts, turkeys, and everything you like.

I think this is the best way to cook steaks, searing so fast the juices cannot escape. I prefer Delmonico steaks, but even fillets stay moist. As the brick oven cools, there is time to cook full meals, side dishes, desserts, and breads. And with residual heat, slow cooking and smoking opportunities abound.

Godspeed,
Walt

Built Like a Brick Oven,
and what a rear chimney!

INTRODUCTION

My desire was to build a brick oven for general but frequent family cooking—family to me includes friends and neighbors. I wanted a large oven like the one my grandfather used; his was made of stone and was exceptionally huge by today's standards, but then again, he had twelve children. His stone oven was located ten feet from the kitchen porch for safety reasons, but I wanted a brick oven that sat on our deck and under the roof so we could cook regardless of weather conditions.

Traditional brick ovens have a top chimney venting out of the front, and such a design interferes with placement under or near a roof. I redesigned the traditional front chimney brick oven design using a horizontal flue pipe that flows the exhaust straight back over the entire oven, running vertically at the rear of the oven. The horizontal flue pipe then works as a "superheater," helping heat the oven more quickly. The traditional European design with the chimney at the front and traveling straight up is still incorporated in my design; however, I turn the flue pipe ninety degrees and run it horizontally straight back over the top of the brick oven. This design allows the incorporation of a flue damper to control or stop flow when you're cooking bread and the oven is sealed off.

Does a horizontal flue pipe work? Yes, it does. Many of us have forgotten or do not know about the coal cylinder stoves. For more than a hundred years, these coal and wood stoves were built with a combustion chamber firebox and top-exhaust hot flue gas vent, but the hot gases

1

were diverted 180 degrees, turning the flue gas straight down to the bottom of the stove. At the bottom, there was another 180-degree turn straight back up to the top, a ninety-degree turn to the house chimney, and another ninety degrees up the chimney. All this was designed to extract more heat from the flue gas. The design was very efficient and was used on most coal furnaces—it was called the lung or kidney. All these heat extraction features are in use today.

Exhaust smoke can travel anywhere you need it to when there is sufficient draft to pull it through, so all that is required is a final chimney height that creates a good draft. The point is don't worry about a short horizontal flue run to get the chimney away from your existing roof.

The second thing that you will notice in my design is that I incorporated a sixteen-by-sixty-inch work ledge that is very convenient. If you can make yours larger, I advise you to do so, as it is a valuable workspace.

This book is intended to be your starting point by giving ideas, so read through it once or twice, trying to remember where you were when you nodded off. Sketch out your designs, and if you can lay out several ideas or plans and then combine the best attributes of each, using an eraser is easier than chipping out block or concrete. There are many websites and web-posted pictures of what others have done, what they forgot, or mistakes they have made. Pick and choose styles, designs, and layouts that will best work for you and print them out. If you cannot draw, then circle the ideas and parts that you like and allow the mason to work them into your design.

CONCEPTUALIZE YOUR DESIGN

If you bring the design into your house, you will have to check and comply with local building codes. But this is where the over-the-oven superheater flue and rear chimney help you bring the brick oven onto your porch or patio, or even into your kitchen. During the startup, if the weather is humid or cold, some smoke can escape the front outside arch, so I recommend building a chimney 10 to 20 percent higher than the minimum required by code to get a good draft. The general rule, and often the regulation, is to keep the top of your new chimney at least ten feet from any adjacent roof. Are you integrating your brick oven into or onto your existing deck/patio? If so, some simple hand sketches will be enough to get you started and determine how much in supplies you will be needing.

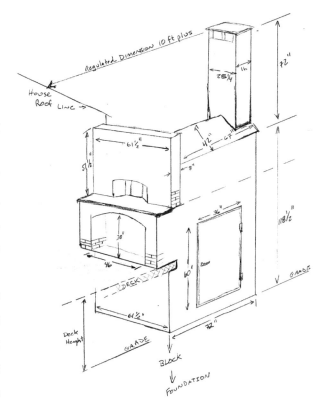

You must first select a footprint. What size will work for you? What quantities of materials will you need? This is best left to you and not really that hard to figure out. At the end of the book, I will have a short materials calculation sheet for you. This can be done by simply looking at various brick oven designs, photographs, websites, etc. and taking ideas from various designs and combining them.

The most commonly built oven size is the 32" x 36" oven; this is the outside dimension and is a very good and workable size. It does not require too much wood or time to heat and is a good family size that can also be used for parties and entertaining.

The oven I built and heavily photographed for your reference has an inside or available cooking area of 36" wide by 48" deep. The outside dimensions of the oven's firebrick are 46" x 58". It heats up within an hour and a half for fast cooking; after that, we are heat soaking the concrete mass.

It really helps to draw it out on paper, or purchase full-size firebricks and lay them out using the bricks themselves—this is what is done for the oven itself. There are two types of firebrick: thick and thin. We only used the thick. There are also two qualities of firebrick: medium and fine. You can use either for the walls and arch, but try to get smooth firebrick for the hearth; there is no price difference. As things go for me, the only firebrick I could find was the medium. It works, but the smooth looks nicer.

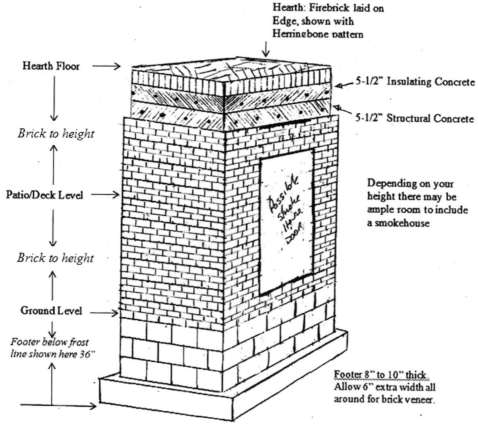

Hearth: Firebrick laid on Edge, shown with Herringbone pattern

Hearth Floor →

5-1/2" Insulating Concrete

5-1/2" Structural Concrete

Brick to height

Patio/Deck Level →

Depending on your height there may be ample room to include a smokehouse

Brick to height

Ground Level →

Footer below frost line shown here 36"

Footer 8" to 10" thick. Allow 6" extra width all around for brick veneer.

This is an arbitrary base; it is illustrated as being 10 feet tall. But remember, three feet is in the ground, and the hearth cooking surface is at a working level of about 40 inches, so this leaves about 44 inches of deck height. Your deck may be two feet off the ground, and that may make an excellent wood storage cove. Or your deck may be eight feet off the ground with plenty of room for a smokehouse.

Before you decide how big your footer will be, you need to decide how big you want your oven and how much insulating concrete you desire to pour around it. A minimum of six inches of insulating concrete surrounding the oven firebox is okay, and that makes the walls 10½" thick. There are many discussions about selecting a proper thickness, and a well-built oven is, by definition, thick-walled. What we are talking about is ample thickness to retain heat for many hours or even days. A poorly built oven would use a minimum of material but would require continual firing and short cooking cycles. Lay out your designs in positions that give a thick, 12"–16" floor, 8"–10" wall, and 12"–16" ceiling, allowing an additional half-inch air gap on each side and on the top. This is required to allow for thermal growth of the brick oven.

When stacking wall thickness dimensions, remember the hearth floor firebrick will be laid in a rowlock position (on their sides), the oven wall will be laid as Soldiers (on their ends), and the ceiling will be laid as a rowlock arch (on their sides).

There are numerous books and sources of information regarding brick oven designs. The oven works by direct-fired radiant heat (a live fire) and residual or retained heat. For this to work well the height of the ceiling should not be too tall or too short. So what does that mean? Nothing really, other than a short ceiling will radiate more heat to your food. So if you choose to cook only thin-crust pizzas, that is a good design. However, if you want to cook big chunks of meat or turkeys, or bake bread loaves, a short ceiling will burn the top. If the ceiling is too high, it will take much longer to bake the top of food. It appears that 16" is a good height, but my arch is 17" at the inside peak, and that seems to work really well as a practical matter. When the oven is cooking at 875°F, an inch or two makes no difference.

Larger ovens such as this could work with a 15" middle peak, but the main reason I wanted the height of 17" was so I could crawl around inside the oven to do maintenance in 50 years—not really, I wanted to be able to cook a big turkey. If the ceiling height was only 15", that would close in the door opening and exclude me from entering, let alone having a little room to bend and twist. This should add very little weight in your decision, because I really doubt that any maintenance will have to be done. If it does, it can be done with the end of a stick or pole.

There are many discussions on the perfect width-to-length dimensions. Some say the perfect ratio is 4:7 (57%) and some say 2:3 (67%); okay, so it's 62% by average. Yet, many preassembled ovens are round, so who really cares? What you are really interested in is available cooking area and fitting it to your home. The available cooking area is the remaining footprint of the floor available to cook while hot coals are burning on the other side.

If you are not sure about the details of your particular situation, don't let it stop you. Lay it out on paper and then, prior to building the next step, make a mock-up and determine your options. As you go you will probably make several mock-ups that allow you to modify and improve your plan. This is the beauty of working with real masons: they will have many ideas and suggestions. And yes, when you are finished, you will no doubt be able to build a better brick oven the second time around, and when you are finished, people will ask you for help. So herein, I hope to convey to you my ideas, mistakes, thoughts, and observations.

Godspeed,
Walt

BUILD IT

Do it yourself or hire a mason—either of you has more information and technology than some Poznan village cook in Poland in 2,000 BC who built up what he could from a pile of rocks and whatever mortar or clay he could find. From that point we are just making the oven more aesthetically pleasing and modernizing it. I got help from a local bricklayer, Doug Walt, and he promised not to charge me extra for my hand in helping him. He did the bulk of the concrete, block, and brickwork; I did some specialty stuff: forming, some bricklaying, arch work, building, and some finish work. The great thing about hiring a bricklayer is that they have all the tools, scaffolding, and material supplies, and most have experience building fireplaces, which saves us all time. And they have many good ideas. But you certainly can do it yourself; it's a time-management issue.

You probably have shovels, a wheelbarrow, mortarboards, trowels, a rubber mallet, a brick-layer's hammer, levels, mason's strings, pointers, a mortar brush, a basic tool bag, and assorted hand and power tools. Depending on the final height of your oven and its chimney, you may need scaffolding, and that can be rented.

For do-it-yourselfers, consider renting a cement mixer to save your back; otherwise, you'll need a mixing trough, and that will slow you down. This is when I decided to enlist the help of a professional because he had the mixer, all the tools, scaffolding, and experience. And between the two of us, we had enough time.

I should also mention government warnings. You may need a permit for building your brick oven depending on its location and the local building codes, and some municipalities require hold-point inspections for chimneys. I can only recommend that if you need a building permit, see if you can mark it "for farm use" to avoid over regulation.

Once you have your oven's footprint determined (for example: 32" x 36", 36" x 36", or 36" x 48"), you must stack up the wall thicknesses, allowing 8" on each side for block and at least 6" on each side for the brick (the brick is 4" and the insulating space is 2"). This increases the footer by 28" both ways, so a 36" x 36" oven needs at least a 64" x 64" footer. Allow more if you are not certain of your final location; it is very cheap to go big here because the form and placement may not be exactly where you think it is.

A little extra room on the footer makes laying the block easier, provides more stability, and gives room to adjust the block and brick edge alignment that is near or under your deck—all this has to be decided early. Take a look at the back cover; the footer and the base lies underneath my deck.

Next and more importantly, laying brick is slow and deliberate slower and straighter is better, take your time, have your materials on hand. This is especially true of the hearth, and all parts of the oven, you may want to knock out a chunk of work due to good weather, but speed will never be remembered a crooked brick will never be forgotten.

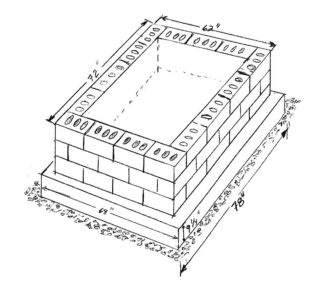

The hole is excavated, a layer of gravel is compressed, a solid footer (using 2" x 8" or 2" x 10") are used, and about three rows of block and one row of brick should be low enough, but check the depth of your frost line.

My chimney rests over the oven, so there was no need to expand the footer. You, however, may want to make the depth larger to accommodate an external chimney. You may also want to consider using bullnose corner blocks for more style. These are stylistic improvements, but my general rule of thumb is to match as much as possible to the design of your house. This provides continuity in design and flow and less of the "afterthought" as a descriptor.

Dig out the foundation to below the frost line; here in this part of Pennsylvania, we use a depth of 36". The slab should be 8" thick or more; 2" x 8" or 2" x 10" used lumber is adequate for the form. Make sure the form is level on all four sides. Lay in 5/8" rebar running on 9" centers, perpendicular running both ways. A trick here is to drill ¾" holes on center in one direction and then drill the opposing ¾" holes 5/8" above center so the rebar touch but do not interfere with each other. Pour the concrete, and smooth and level the top with a two-by-four.

Let the foundation cure five days or longer, then pull off the forms, chalk a squared outline for the concrete block, and use a plumb bob to get a true vertical position. Set up square chalk lines and start laying the block; be sure to make allowances for future brick veneering. Also, as the first row is laid, verify the line of block and future brick edge to assure alignment with the deck/patio edge.

Concrete blocks are made of Portland cement and aggregates (sands and gravel), so a good, high-strength Portland cement mix is fine; just ask for high-strength sack mix. I stuff rebar in the corners and fill with a cement-gravel mixture for added strength.

The block wall will come about 36" to grade level plus whatever height you need to come up to your patio or deck elevation and then an additional 26" to the top of the block (26" + 5.5" concrete support slab + 5.5" concrete insulating slab + 5" firebrick hearth ~ 42"). Please refer to our foundation figure above and adjust your drawing as necessary. You may have room for wood storage or a dedicated ash pit.

Foundation is dug to 40" below the local frost line. My concrete deck is about five feet above grade, putting the oven hearth at 102" above ground, giving ample room for a brick smokehouse underneath. I will skip the foundation building because so much has been printed or is available on the web already, but it is nothing more than four walls and a door, if you wish.

At this point, you have poured the footer and have built up the concrete layers to the correct height; I omitted the drawings because your design will be different. Nonetheless leave it cure for five or more days. So we will skip ahead to the installation of the structural concrete floor.

This is the inside of my smokehouse. I am shoring up a wood bottom to pour a concrete slab above it, which is now thirty-some inches above my concrete deck. The stainless steel bars above are for hanging meats for smoking. The OSB or plywood and two-by-four supports are used to hold the first 5½" structural concrete floor or slab in place until the concrete cures (seven days). Make sure you have enough support under the temporary floor so the concrete does not sag. This is the structural concrete floor, which is poured over most of the block walls, less a ¾" lip. You will notice below that I am using 1" x 6" lumber set on the edge of the concrete block. After the framing is removed, this ¾" space will be sufficient enough to allow for thermal expansion, and you can see how I offset the rebar holes 5/8" to prevent interference. The concrete floors will be inside and not touching the outside brick walls.

What you are looking at above is a gray scrap piece of OSB or plywood. It is gray from mixing brick mortar on it. This is the temporary floor and the same OSB/plywood that is supported underneath with two-by-four studs. Frame the first structural floor and insulating concrete slabs in the same manner, using 1" x 6" lumber. The rebar is 5/8" and set about every 9" (between 6" and 10" will work). In the upper right hand corner, I notched out an area for the 4" square steel smokehouse chimney. Also notice that the hearth's base and all oven parts are at least 1½" from the outside brick. This must be done to allow for an air gap and thermal expansion. After this structural support slab cures, you will pour another 5½" thick vermiculite (insulating) slab on top of it, giving it an 11" thick base.

Above is a close-up of the ash dump framing. The ash dump is formed with scrap wood, screwed to the OSB/plywood temporary floor, and located near the oven's front. An ash dump is not necessary, but it is convenient. The form of the ash dump is just a simple, wooden box sized to a standard ash dump door that's available at your local block and cement company. In the picture above, the first 5½" layer of concrete has been poured, and the ash dump is inside the block. In the picture below of the second concrete slab—the insulating concrete slab—you will notice that I tilted the ash dump box to bring the ash dump closer to the front of the oven.

These are the two support layers. The bottom layer is structural, high-strength concrete, and the top layer will be a vermiculite concrete layer, providing insulation between this and the bottom. The rebar is on 9" centers and has a 5/8" diameter. The 1" x 6" boards must be removed, and that space must be filled with free-flowing vermiculite and diatomaceous earth (swimming pool earth).

11

Close in front you will notice the form for the ash dump. In the rear, you will notice a red 4" square pipe. This is the smokehouse vent, or chimney, and is just an option. If you have the height and can incorporate a smokehouse under your brick oven, then install a chimney. You can cut one in as I have in the far corner so as not to take up oven space, or you may prefer an external chimney; both will work well, and an external chimney may look better. Either way, try to blend it with the same architecture of your house.

Above is a closer look into the ash dump hole. Each slab may have its own angle, and although it seems complicated, all you must do is make a simple box that represents the void or shoot. In my design, and only because of the placement of the smokehouse below it, I centered the ash dump between the two center smokehouse hanging bars located underneath the very first structural layer of concrete. At the second insulating layer, I brought that position over to the center of the oven doors. Once the concrete cured I simply knocked out the wood.

The picture above is underneath the first concrete structural support slab after the plywood and supports were removed. On the left is the ash dump shoot. On the underside, it is centered so it would clear the inside brick of the smokehouse and fall between two smokehouse hanging rods. If you do not have a smokehouse underneath, then the ash dump can fall anywhere inside.

Many brick oven builders/owners elect not to build the ash dump. This is a matter of preference and has no impact on cooking or baking. **Only note that installing an ash dump afterward will nearly be impossible and it certainly will be time consuming, whereas if you put an ash dump in and you do not like it, then it can easily be filled in with concrete.**

The smokehouse is just a box with a venthole in the far back corner that I bring up behind the hearth and brick oven; the venthole is just a 4" x 4" space. Later, an adjustable damper will be installed to control smoke and heat flow. A separate 3" elbow and 3" downcomer pipe will be installed to ensure adequate heat control in the smoke zone. The bottom of the downcomer pipe will be the first part of the chimney and will be at least 6" higher than the inlet air pipe.

Both concrete base layers have been poured and rest on the interior block walls. After the wood forms are removed, a gap is visible (this gap must remain) between the brick oven and the outside or façade brick. So do not allow excess mortar or brick chips to fill the gap as this may bind later and crack the brick façade. This open area gap allows for thermal expansion; however it can be loosely filled with a high temperature insulating material. The oven will reach 1,200°F with wood and 1,450°F with coal. Concrete expands about 0.007" per degree, so this five-foot oven could expand 3/16" or more. Below is a glimpse of the wood storage area, and to the lower right the smokehouse door is visible.

The exterior front has been brought out 16" onto my concrete deck. This area will provide space for wood storage and support for a work shelf; eventually it will support a piece of 18"-wide granite. The granite will rest on the brick but will not touch the concrete or firebrick; a gap will separate them to prevent the granite from cracking. The loose block and firebrick are solely being used to temporarily hold the wooden arch.

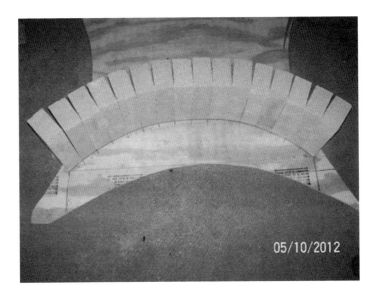

ARCH WORK

Think about the interface of your oven and your deck, or discuss with your builder. If your deck is wood, then you may not want all this weight sitting on top of it, unless there is concrete block and brick directly underneath it. My concrete blocks are laid under the concrete deck and from there up, on the outside, a single layer of brick is raised (this is shown behind the wood storage area and under the front part of two concrete slabs).

Use bricks to lay out arches to achieve a good, tight fit and symmetry. The images above and below are an example of the wood storage arch, and the dry-run layout will show you how many bricks will be needed across it. The same process is used for each arch, using the brick of that arch. You may have to add or subtract a brick, or you may have to raise or lower the arch to get a better fit. On this oven the wood storage area is 46" wide and, at its peak, is 30" high. The outside oven door is 29½" wide x 11½" high. The inside oven door is 16½" wide x 12¾" tall. The brick oven arches were 37" wide x 17¼" high—these require a brick overhang of ½" per side for support.

In the photo above there are four plywood arches cut out and screwed together with two-by-four spacers to cover the depth of the firewood storage cove. The spacers are set so that two plywood arches are under each brick; this is two bricks deep (about 16"). The plywood arches are temporarily shored up with block, brick, and wood wedges, and then the countertop in front of the oven is bricked and the corners are filled with scrap brick. This area is NOT under the oven; it sits completely out in front of the oven.

A ¼" layer of fire clay mortar is laid down on the vermiculite concrete. Then the large (2.5" x 4.5" x 9") firebricks are laid out for the hearth. Normally, these are laid straight, but I have chosen a herringbone pattern because it looks nicer and the hardware (flat iron skillets and bread/pizza peels) should glide across it freely. This, of course, requires cutting extra brick but it's a nicety that shows you have put in that extra effort.

The exterior front has been brought out 16" onto my deck. This provides a nice work shelf and will support a piece of 18"-wide granite with a 2" overhang, and for me the larger the work top the better. I was only limited by the size of some leftover granite. Remember, neither the outside brick façade wall nor the granite can touch any hot surface of the oven.

THE HEARTH

The firebricks for the hearth are installed, and now the solders are laid out to determine the outline of the oven. If you are patterning yours after this design, it is a large if not commercial-size oven. Most household ovens are smaller and will require much less wood and time to heat up. However this oven can cook up to eight pizzas at one time or 16 loaves of bread at one time. It will eventually require 333 firebricks, whereas a normal oven may only take 180 firebricks.

We cut in the ash dump and formed the hearth around it using a standard ash dump door available at any concrete supply company. The thickness of the cast iron for the ash dump is slightly less than ¼", so this depth is cut into the brick edges as an inset with a 4" diamond wheel. If you notice, these firebrick are course-grain and were the only ones available to me at the time, but no sooner than I laid the floor, I found fine grain and smooth firebrick. The course-grain works fine, but the fine-grained firebrick would have made a nicer-looking floor; at 900°F it really doesn't matter much.

The solders have been laid out and fire clay mortared to the hearth floor. There is only mortar on the bottom and on the outside at the corners, and this means there is no mortar on the inside. Your oven can be laid out however you wish, but mine has curved edges on all four "corners." I did this to keep the fire and heat rolling around with good flow. Many ovens have a very simple, flat back, which works fine, but the rounded corners are easier to clean and look more professional in my opinion.

This is the front of the oven (at the top). **Note that the oven façade wraps around the front but never touches the hearth or any part of the oven's firebrick floor or walls. These two must always be separated; otherwise, severe cracking will occur.**

The blue foam arch is for the inside oven door. It is 16½" wide and 12¾" tall. This size allows a 15-pound turkey access. The inside oven door (pattern shown) will have a different arch than the outside door arch, with the outside oven door arch being flatter and lower and the inside oven door being higher and narrower. Keeping the outside door lower than the oven door forces the smoke up the chimney. Arch supports need to remain in place for four to five days until the mortar cures completely, so do not rush to remove them. Pulling out the foam arch support too early could mean that your mortar will crack and you'll need a do-over, or you may weaken the joint and not know it until the oven is fired, which then leads to big problems. Please wait it out, because the clay-based mortar does not reach full strength until it is fired by slowly heating it, so the dry (no heat) cure period is more important.

I use 2" foam board to form arches because it is strong and wide enough to hold the brick. While you are cutting the brick, take the time to bevel the front and inside bottoms. Notice how the outside façade is separated with temporary cardboard inserts (on each side of the door). This is to keep a clear gap between the hot firebrick and the cold outside. If the cardboard was not placed there, mortar could fall into the gap and cause a hard link between a hot oven on the move and a cold wall not intended to move.

This is the outside façade arch, and behind it is the firebrick oven arch. The distance between the two arches is about 8" and between and above them will be the top front exit for the oven's chimney. This outside arch is flatter and lower than the oven arch and yes, up to this point, this is a traditional brick oven.

THE FAÇADE

Most ovens do not have a chimney damper, but this brick oven is designed for your porch or deck, so I wanted a way to close off any cold air from the chimney when not in use (so dampers are not the norm but add value).

The front countertop will sit above the wood storage arch. Between that arch and the top flat where the granite will be set, we filled in with scrap bricks, hardened mortar, and stone chips.

09/10/2012

A side view shows the air gap required, because the cooler façade and the hot oven must be separated to allow room for thermal growth. Defect and scrap bricks are used for inside (not visible) supports to hold the chimney firebrick in place as internal sidewalls. A 1/4" to 3/16" gap is left all around the chimney damper, and that gap is filled with sand so no mortar drops in.

This photograph looks up between the front façade entry (to the right) and the oven firebrick entry (to the left). You can see the damper mechanism above and between. This inside arch is slightly higher than the outside arch to allow for proper venting up and out and to reduce smoke exiting the front arch onto your porch. On the left and right sides the external façade is brought in on an angle to within ¼" to 3/8" of the oven's front wall with no contact between them.

This picture is from the inside of the oven looking outward. **Note that I tapered the inside bottom of the arch to help the combustion exhaust roll out exit the oven. You will also see that the final brick solders, which line up against both sides of the oven front wall, are a bit short but not enough to cut another and insert a sliver of a brick, so a little extra mortar was used at the oven's front wall on both sides.**

Below and on the right side you will see the back of the oven wall with two rounded corners. You can place these "corner" solders in whatever radius you need to work with your brick dimensions.

The oven must not be too high or too short; normally 16" is the height, but here 17" is used as the maximum. The arch height and width is laid out with a complete set of firebricks that are adjusted to give ½" overhang on each side. A plywood template is made, and it is used to cut out numerous 2" wide blue foam insulation boards. That will be 1" narrower so that it fits into the solder walls.

THE OVEN CEILING ARCH

You will also see the very first blue arch form (on the left). It is set at the inside beveled arch of the oven door. Next is a transition arch, which is the average arch of the door arch and the oven ceiling arch; all the arches are spaced fairly close. If you enjoy woodworking, then use wood as either can be removed easily.

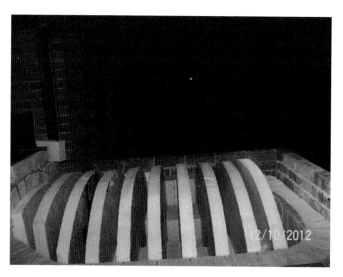

This oven is 36" wide (on the inside dimension), giving me a nice curve using a full 18 bricks to span 37", allowing ½" overset so the arch can rest on the solders. The length is 48" long (on the inside dimension), and you can see that each ceiling endcap will be tapered down to the solders. Normally, the back wall is made straight, but I wanted the heat from the fire to roll forward. All center foam arches must be cut identically—having a tiny little low spot or tiny high spot will be magnified when you look into a completed oven. You have one shot at doing this correctly, so please take your time.

The bottom row is wedged in place and set back a ½". After all the foam boards have been cut, lay out a couple rows of dry (non-mortared) brick to ensure that the initial layout is working properly. Irregularities will occur in the brick, so the forms must be exact in order to maintain good joints. You also do not want to cut any brick to fit into the top of the arch, but if you have to, it will not hurt the strength. Dry fitting twice is better than having irregular gaps.

Note that almost no mortar is used on the inside edge, but the mortar is used at the backside creating a wedge shape. I opted to alternate the bricks so that every other row starts with a half brick. This technique will increase the structural integrity of the arch.

We also started at both sides and worked our way in. This allows the brick to be self-supporting, but for some reason at the top midpoint (high noon), we had to trim the middle top row to get a tighter fit. This was a pain in rump roast even with a good diamond tip bit. It wasn't what I wanted, but we trimmed the center brick to make a tighter fit. To avoid this center-sliced wedge problem, in lieu of starting at both sides and working toward the middle, there may be a way to work from one side and then adjust the very last brick row on the outside wall by adjusting the amount of mortar or the final wedge brick. If this can be done your ceiling will be neater.

This is the front of the oven. The domed arch is being tied into the front wall with a slight downward slope. This allows the smoke and heat to roll back as needed and flow out of the oven. This is not needed, but it does help reflect heat and looks nicer too.

The main arch is complete. This is the back end (**note the smokehouse chimney**). Two firebricks will be used and set on or near 45° angles to give an arch at the top of the back end. After the arch is complete, the entire top is buttered with mortar up to ½" thick and not thicker—this will help hold the firebrick in place and the thin (less than ½") mortar will crack where it needs to crack without comprising and cracking the firebrick. There is *no* mortar between the oven and outside wall—the oven must float; at 1,400°F, it will expand about 5/32" from the middle.

All front bricks cut and laid on a decline are mortared into the inside front wall. This gives an important angle that allows heat to reflect back into the oven and directs smoke downward and outward to the chimney. If you cannot figure out how to do this tapered step, go straight; the oven will work nonetheless. A slight butter layer of mortar is used for surety, a back grip if you will.

This is the back wall. All the back bricks cut and laid out on a decline are mortared into place. These angled bricks sit atop the solders and allow the heat to rise and reflect back into the oven, and the heat and smoke to roll across the top of the oven.

This is the backside on a corner. The larger bricks are cut and trimmed to fit as you can best fit them into place. The last brick is the hardest to fit, or at least is seemed so, but smaller and smaller pieces can be cut and mortared into place until the bricks have made it past the domed arch (meaning they will be out of sight).

The picture above is the finished back of the dome. After the first angled bricks were laid, we had room to insert V-cut brick wedges in between the dome and the angled brick. Inserting these helped fill the gap and make the whole dome stronger. Next, ¾" plywood was placed around the outside wall to prepare for covering the oven dome with vermiculite concrete, the insulating concrete layer.

Prior to pouring vermiculite, I used high-temperature thermal expanding foam between the oven refractory hearth floor and the outer cold façade bricks to ensure no mortar dropped between them. I used this because the foam is pliable and will move with the oven's thermal growth and contraction.

This area is located in front of the oven's ash dump at the façade's front archway. The foam heat insulation is used to fill a gap between the inside hot oven and the not-so-hot brick façade.

The rough concrete is above the arch, and this weight of the concrete helps secure that arch. It eventually will be covered with a piece of granite that will NOT touch any other brick, especially the firebrick; it will float and be completely insulated from anything that can thermally move.

To help secure the oven dome, it is covered with a thin coat of mortar; you can actually see the brick mortar joint indentations underneath it. Any top and side coating less than ½" should be sufficient to help secure it, but not too thick to prevent or cause thermal mechanical expansion and cracking of the oven brick.

The ¾" OSB or plywood is then formed on the inside walls and will prevent the vermiculite concrete from touching the outside walls. The OSB/plywood is all angled and wedged for easy removal. A lot of space is needed (at least one inch) because the concrete will soak into and expand the plywood. And remember that the larger the plywood pieces, the harder they will be to remove.

This is the overly discussed aluminum foil layer. It has one purpose: separate two layers of concrete—that is it. Why? To prevent the massive top layers of insulated concrete from cracking the brick dome. It does not provide insulation; it does not provide a moisture barrier; nor does it help hold or reflect the heat inside. It separates the first thin layer of mortar from the secondary and tertiary layers of vermiculite concrete so those outside heavy layers do not adhere to the thin mortar layer, which would expand and crack the firebrick. The 6" wire mesh helps keep the vermiculite concrete together, but the reality is that these large masses of concrete will crack when thermally expanded, and they will crack anything that is attached.

The ¾" OSB/plywood is built completely around the oven, so at no point will it come into contact with the outside brick wall.

The layers of vermiculite concrete are made into a "fluffy" mix: ½ bag of mortar, sand, and some gravel with ½ bag of vermiculite. How much is too much vermiculite? The concrete seems to be able to absorb only so much and that is the stopping point; we poured it in until it wouldn't take more without drying out the concrete mix. This is a great place to throw in your scrap or damaged bricks, gravel, and that horrific coffee mug given to you from Aunt Martha, as the corners require a lot of filler. Just don't throw in any combustible materials or materials with moisture.

My oven has four layers of vermiculite concrete covering it, which increases the total oven weight to 4 tons. It's good in that once it's hot, it stays hot. But it does take time to heat soak the 8,800-pound oven; cooking can begin within two hours and the heat soaking requires four or more hours. A smaller oven would not require as much soak time, but it may not stay hot for days. As the outside walls are laid, vermiculite and diatomaceous earth (pool filter earth) are used as dynamic thermal insulating filler between the oven and the external walls. If you have any holes or gaps, the vermiculite will find them and drain out.

Above is a first look inside the oven dome with all the foam removed. Some clay mortar needs to be cleaned up, and once fired, it will turn whiter and match the firebrick. The inside dimensions are 36" wide by 48" deep. The dome height is 17" at the peak. The area looks somewhat rough, but that may be due to the lighting and shadows from the camera flash—the oven surfaces are rather smooth. In a couple areas, I was able to regrout with clay mortar to get a better joint.

I left this "dry" for a few days, but clay mortar requires heat to cure. Fortunately, I was able to crawl inside and touch up some areas. But this is not recommended without a "fire watch," as this is a confined space. But hey, my wife promised to pull me out if I got stuck. Don't worry about being able to get into your oven; any touch-up work can be done with the end of a long stick or dowel rod with a flattened end.

On the left is the outside or façade brick, which extends up to the oven but does not touch it. It is the tapered wall in the top middle of this picture. On the right side under the arch is the entryway into the oven. Please notice that no part of the outside façade brick touches the brick oven. Eventually, you will stuff black flexible furnace gaskets between the outside façade and oven walls.

In the above picture, you see the flat, top surface of the external and internal oven arches. This is level and where I elected to install a damper.

THE FLUE AND HORIZONTAL CHIMNEY

The damper is cast steel and will grow thermally quite a bit, and at different rates than concrete or brick. Due to the expansion differential, sand is used as an expansion joint all around it. Sand is packed all around the damper between the brick to ensure that it has room to move when heated and that no mortar or brick will touch it.

I opted to use the external turn-screw drive and not the internal manual gear lever. Either is fine, but the internal gear lever would not be visible, whereas the turn-screw will be visible.

This oven is designed to sit inside our elevated deck, so my front chimney rises up as any traditional European brick oven would; however, it will immediately make a 90° turn and run straight across the top of the oven, working as a superheater to heat the oven a little faster. But more importantly for me, it takes the heat and smoke to a rear chimney located five feet away from my deck and roof.

The first chimney pipe is placed on its side for the first horizontal run. It has a square cutout with a small 4" diamond wheel cutter and sits directly over top of the damper.

The horizontal flue pipe is set on a very slight incline, ½" per foot, but can be laid flat. An incline (in either direction) will allow moisture to drain out. The lower right-hand side of the photo is located directly above the damper. Refractory bricks are used to secure the open end. We had a few extra, so we used them just as supports and guides. One per side would be enough or just use extra mortar; these are mortared on the bottom but not to the flue pipe. The façade of the oven has not been laid yet, but it will be bricked up against the firebrick, blocking the flue pipe (those located at the date stamp).

The brick oven façade is bricked to the header of the deck's trusses. It is two bricks thick, solid, and mortared together, so no smoke will ever reach the deck's header. This is the inside wall and will not be visible from the deck (oven front), or even from the yard. Some leftover fire-bricks are used around the flue pipe as guides and as the mortar sets it will be neatly pointed.

The flue gases go up through the damper, a very short vertical run of chimney (just enough to get past the damper's swinging door), and then to where the chimney first goes horizontal. We put this on a slight angle, just for moisture control, but it can be straight across, or even downward sloping, if you want moisture to drain toward the chimney and away from the oven.

This is the top of the horizontal run of flue pipe. The oven brick arch is covered by vermiculated concrete, and we have placed a few bricks over it to bring it into the chimney. The piece of plastic on the right-hand side is covering our 4" square steel smokehouse chimney. All of the flue pipe and oven will be covered with another thick layer of insulating concrete.

The flue pipes are extended across the whole oven over to the rear chimney. This is a two-flue chimney with the chimney flue on the far left for the smokehouse (located under the brick oven) and the chimney on the right for the brick oven chimney. I used 6" round flue pipe over the 4" square smokehouse pipe. The white powder is the diatomaceous earth and vermiculite insulation mixed together and used to separate the oven from the outside brick façade.

I wasn't kidding—it was early November when I crawled into the oven and inspected all the mortar joints. This step is not necessary or even safe, but I wanted to clean up some areas and butter-up some joints so they looked better. I am a big guy, 225 pounds and six feet tall, but I managed to get in and do the entire cleanup. As a result, I now know that there is room to do any possible maintenance work in the future. Since this is a confined space, I did have a "hole watch," my lovely wife Roxanne, and it's evident that she suppressed any urges to stuff me in the whole way and brick over the oven front.

FIRST HEAT CURE

As seen above, a small curing fire is required initially because the firebricks are laid using fire-clay mortar, which does not cure unless heated. Each day I made a larger fire and left it to burn out. By the end of the week, I had a good-sized fire going and the slow process cured the mortar without any cracking problems.

In the photograph above, the front wall is two bricks deep (solid), and behind the open area are two firebricks that butt up against the fluepipe's 90° turn. I left this open while I had a piece of granite carved out with our family name and wine label on it. This oven is 61¾" wide by 94" high. At the bottom of the wood storage area, we placed two 1"-thick stones as a base cover for the exposed brick.

The rear chimney is complete with a cap and two flues. This particular chimney design is consistent with our other chimneys (we have four double-flue chimneys at our house and garage, so I wanted continuity with the other chimneys). The horizontal flue pipe is covered with vermiculite concrete to act as an insulator in helping to keep the heat inside and heat the top of the oven as the hot flue gases exit across its top. The beauty of this is that the oven can sit up on your porch and the chimney is five feet away. Code tends to dictate that the height of the chimney be at least ten feet <u>away from</u> any adjacent roof. This is a good minimum, but anything further away (which means higher) just works better.

From any lumber supply yard, you can get metal studs and metal roofing. Using a channel, we built a metal roof and screwed it into the mortar joints with blue concrete screws. The roof is small and can be made of concrete, tiles, slate, or any noncombustible material. I used simple steel roofing used for barns and pole buildings, as it is inexpensive and, more importantly, because you can purchase it in very small amounts. There are fancy metal roofing materials, but most must be purchased in very large quantities. If you don't want to do this work, the lumberyard can provide you with names of roofers that will do it for you. One difficult area to see is that the vermiculite concrete joint at each wall can leak smoke; you will notice this as you are drying your oven. I poured a liquid, high-temperature sealant across the joint to seal it.

Simple metal roofing was installed and flashed on both sides (front side and chimney side).

Here is typical flashing installed and later caulked with brown silica. A vented ridge cap was installed to allow any excess heat or moisture to escape.

THE WOOD DOOR

This is the brick oven door used to hold heat in for baking breads and sealing the oven for the next day's use. I made the brick oven door by using the original 2" foam arch pattern. I traced the 2" foam onto 1/16" sheet steel and 2" thick ceramic insulation block I purchased from Chiz Brothers in West Elizabeth, PA.

The outside is white oak and appears to be a raised-panel door, but it is not a true panel; the doorframe has a simple rabbit cut on the inside. The panel just floats inside the wooden doorframe with its own rabbit cut. The inside of the wood is stained and painted with sodium silicate, a fire retardant. The blue ceramic insulation is screwed into the wood and then the plate steel is screwed into the blue ceramic. The blue ceramic is not food grade, so the steel cladding on the front protects the food and then the whole thing is painted with heavy-duty, black, high-temperature furnace paint. The black paint encapsulates the ceramic fibers. The whole ceramic block can be incased in steel if you wish and are good with tin work.

The wrought iron handles are stock ordered online.

Above is a side view of the door. To the left is the white oak, saturated with sodium silicate and then dried. There is a 2"-thick slab of ceramic insulation covered by a piece of sheet metal. This design holds the heat in and fits snuggly up against the inside the arch of the oven door—the door's arches were formed using the same 2" arch foam board used to form the brick arch, so they are identical arches. The wood is ½" taller and each side extends ½" to form a cover lip.

This is the nearly finished oven, with some slate added to the bottom of the wood storage cove. Then I stucco-finished the back of the wood storage cove, making it darker. The granite top is installed and does not touch the brick wall; it does contour back into and nearly up against the oven's firebrick all at the same level. Since granite is much thinner than brick, we had to cut and add a thin brick underneath the granite. If you look closely, you will see those bricks are thin. We had one small piece of granite left, and we sent that to the local tombstone engraver with our private wine label "Vinoski." He cut it in and layered it with gold.

This is outside of the smokehouse. The brick oven sits above it, but the two are completely separated. The metal door and frame were ordered locally and made to size, 3' x 5'.

IT ALL WORKS OUT

At first I calculated a need for 290 firebricks to build a brick oven. The yard foreman said they were sold on pallets of 300. I asked if he thought any would be cracked and he said no. I said, "Well, hopefully I won't miscut them and have to come back for more."

We ended up with a few extra bricks that we used around the flue and damper. We had one brick left, so Doug tossed it up over his shoulder from the chimney cap and said, "It's gone. No worries." And he was right; it all works out.

And I left to catch another flight, where a guy was chewing on a big fat cigar and you could smell the fresh tobacco throughout the plane. A woman with a small dog was sitting between us on the airplane's emergency exit row. The woman demanded that the guy put away his cigar. They ended up saying a few words until he offered her a compromise. "Look, if you get rid of your dog, I'll get rid of the cigar."

To his surprise, the lady opened the emergency exit door and tossed her dog out. In response, the man threw his cigar out, probably thinking I have other cigars and I have won. However, the woman suddenly pulled on her dog's leash, pulling the dog back in, thinking she had won. Weird I know, but guess what the dog had in its mouth? Yes, you are right, a brick! I know it's an old one, but maybe you can tell it to friends over a good steak cooked in your brick oven.

COOKING AND THE SMOKEHOUSE

Here's a shot of a fired oven with a couple steaks and a whole pork tenderloin. At these temperatures the meat will sear and cook quickly, your meat will be juicy and firm – surely satisfying.

Below is a picture of the smokehouse propane burner assembly purchased from Allied Kenco Sales. It's complete with Robertshaw temperature controls that allow for cold smoking (60°) up to 220°F, and makes great ribs, hams, turkeys, and kielbasa.

I located the Robertshaw propane temperature controller under our concrete deck on the inside of the smokehouse so it would not be degraded by the weather. As shown above, it has a rubber hose connected to a small propane tank that was used to tune the system, get all the bugs worked out, and determine the best placement for the smokehouse thermocouple.

This is the burner assembly and the wood ship pan inside the smokehouse. The small black pipe is the gas pipe; the large black pipe is the inlet air pipe. The smaller hoses and wires are for the Robertshaw controller. The drip pan is available at Wal-Mart in the automotive department. The racks on the right side are used when smoking ribs or chicken.

Low temperature smoking starts with brining the meat, the brining allows a small amount of salt to enter the meat and salts are hydrophobic (attract water) so they tend to pull out some water, but what the salts do is protect the meat from bacteria attack during the cold or warm smoke. I use natural high-mineral content salts (from the sea or from the mine, but not salts that have been stripped of all minerals leaving only sodium chloride (common white table salt).

Mineralized natural salts contain sodium, calcium phosphates, potassium and magnesium, etc. (minerals now known to lower blood pressure and be healthful). Potassium helps to protect against the toxicity of sodium and magnesium deficiency leads to cardiovascular diseases and sudden coronary death. Don't be afraid of mineralize salts, your bones are made of 50% salts, and think about this our bodies only need 4 grams of sodium per day for replacement and they need 0.5 gram of magnesium per day so why strip out the minerals? Don't be 'a-salted' by pure sodium.

EPILOGUE

By now I am hoping your brick oven is working and you were able to incorporate a smokehouse as well. Maybe your smokehouse is beside your oven or behind it; it all can work. It's even possible to take heat out of the unit and transfer it to another room or floor using copper water piping—you can make this as complex as you wish.

Once you have worked the brick oven to its peak firing temperature, cooking can begin. I lay in two straight long barrel staves, and upon them I stack four 18" long logs perpendicularly, pushing them to the back of the oven across the staves. In the front of the oven I use hardwood logs, split in several pieces, then kindling under, and in front I stack the hardware splitters and shavings. There is no need for paper, lighter fuel, or a starter log, however I have tried self-lighting charcoal. The hardwood kindling is all that it takes to get a good fire underway.

I feed the fire for an hour and a half, then I move the wood to one side, and at this point the oven floor is hot and ready for steak (placed on a flat casted iron skillet) and pizzas (tossed in on the hearth itself with no pan). I find it easier to cook around 850°F to 950°F to get good, consistent results. You can of course cook a pizza at 1,250°F, but in very little time it goes from a perfect dish to a burnt offering. I use a DeWalt handheld infrared thermal gun to measure floor and wall temperatures.

As the hearth floor cools (about every twenty minutes), I move the red-hot coals and burning wood to the cool side of the oven, add a log, sweep the floor, and continue cooking on the hot side. I do not worry about some ash dust (it has a pH of 10 and helps neutralize acidic foods), nor do I worry about a little burnt edge; a little carbon acts as a filter sucking up toxins.

Bread cooking is a learned art that took me about five tries to get right. There are many books on baking bread, but in a brick oven the oven must be heated 550°F to 600°F; all coals, wood, and ash must be swept out and the oven door placed on the oven. Bread is spongelike absorbing all the oven smoke and smells, so a clean oven is important. Once all smoldering coals are removed your risen bread can be placed into the oven with a peel and the door set in place sealing in the heat for 20 to 45 minutes or whatever the recipe calls for.

RECIPES

Pizza Dough

4 cups of Double 00 Flour

2 teaspoons mineralized salt

½ teaspoon active yeast

1-½ cups water (if dry add 1 Tablespoon at a time)

Mix well and let rise for 2 hours doubling in size. Roll the dough, roll out the air & cut into 2 or 3 pieces depending on the size of your oven and roll into a ball. Dust with flour and store dough balls in plastic wrap. Dough can be refrigerated for a few days.

Pizza

Pull or stretch the dough ball thin, this Double 00 flour can be spun in the air or roll the dough ball out flat and even. Rolling the dough does make it tough and is frowned apon. Dust the flat well with flour so it does not stick on the peel. The bottom must be dry if one piece sticks to the peel, then only the toppings slide off the peel.

Top with plain tomato sauce, fresh buffalo mozzarella, and drizzle with olive oil.

Depending on the oven temperature it will cook in about 1 or 2 minutes; if your oven is cool it could take much longer. Rotate the pizza if it starts to get dark brown and this can happen in 40 seconds in a hot oven. The cheese should be completely melted and slightly browned pull it out of the oven and dust with fresh oregano and basil.

Pizza – Other Toppings

It is best to keep pizza's simple – having fewer main ingredients but anything you like can be added over the top. Roasted Vegetables, Hams, Steak, and cured meats, (these should be added under the cheese or directly on the sauce as they are dried already and can easily turn very tough, but prosciutto, culatello, salami, capicolla all of these make fine toppings.

White Pizza with Claims

1 can Claims, retain juice
3 tablespoons of white wine
1 Tablespoon minced garlic
2 Tablespoon of Olive Oil
2 Tablespoons of butter
Parsley,
Shredded Parmigianino reggiano & Provolone cheeses

Sauté claims, wine, garlic, olive oil, and butter essentially heating the claims to warm and re-ducing the sauce mixture. Do not overcook the claims and leave a little sauce place this topping on the pizza and sprinkle parsley add a little shredded Parmigianino reggiano and shredded provolone.

White Seafood Pizza

¼ lb Small Shrimp
¼ lb Small Scallops
¼ lb Calamari
3 tablespoons of white wine
2 Tablespoon minced garlic
2 Tablespoon of Olive Oil
2 Tablespoons of butter
Parsley and Oregano
Shredded Parmigianino reggiano, Mozzarella & Provolone cheeses

Sauté shrimp, scallops, calamari, wine, garlic, olive oil, and butter essentially heating until just barely cooked (even slightly raw) leave some sauce mixture. Now distribute mix over one large or two small pizzas and sprinkle parsley and oregano add a little shredded cheeses.

Round Rye Bread

Start your sour dough culture five to seven days prior to making your bread always use rye flour as it does not breakdown like white flour and it has very little gluten. Take a very clean pint jar and mix 2 Tablespoons of whole grain rye flour with 2 Tablespoons of pure water, stir for 30 seconds, mark the level on the jar and let sit out of the sunlight for 1 day. On the second day add a Tablespoon each of rye flour and of water, mark the level on the jar and let stand another day.

On the third day, you'll see more bubbling if not throw it out and start over; if everything is bubbling fine, take out about ½ of the mixture and throw it out, this removes excess alcohol and now add in 3 Tablespoons each of rye flour and water, let stand for 24 hours the fourth day. On day four, throw away 2/3 of the mixture and add 3 tablespoons each of rye flour and water this step allows the acids from the bacteria to build up (souring the starter). Your sourdough starter will be ready on day five. You can maintain the starter in your refrigerator and feed it weekly (remove it from the refrigerator use or dispose of some starter) add fresh rye yeast and water and let it work 12-hours and refrigerate it.

At least day prior to firing your brick oven, remove your sourdough starter to warm up. A 100% rye bread dough can take 24 hours to rise, using ½ rye and ½ wheat still can take 14 hours both breads are very delicious and good for you. Rye has the salts good for our bones: phosphorus, potassium, selenium, manganese, iron, zinc, copper and it makes a pretty good whiskey as well.

Ingredients:
1-3/4 Cups of warm water
1/3 Cup of sourdough starter
2 Tablespoons of Molasses
Flour: Either 1-3/4 Cups or RYE and 1-3/4 Cups of Bread Flour or 3-1/2 Cups of Rye only (this will require 24 rise time)
1-3/4 teaspoons of mineralized salt

Combine in a bowl water, starter and molasses; in another bowl combine flour(s) and salt and slowly stir the dry ingredients into the wet ingredients. Mix and let rest for 15 minutes and repeat (mix and let rest for 15 minutes). Now Proof the Bread by covering with plastic and let the bread rise a warm place (a 50% four mixture will take 12 to 14 hours and a 100% rye mixture will take 24 hours). After this proofing, work the bread slightly and fold the bread into a round bowl, cover with plastic wrap let it rest for 15 minutes and then remove and place a very-well-floured towel into the round bowl for the final rise of 1-1/2 hours. Ensure that your brick oven is at 550°F and clean of all ash and wood and sprayed with water, then place the bread on a well-floured peel, score the top thrice, and put into the brick oven, close the door (or block it with bricks and bake about 20 to 25 minutes or until the bread measures 205°F with a infrared thermometer.

Beef Roast

After you have finished cooking bread your oven will remain warm for a day or longer. I like to cook beef roast it takes 2 hours in a 300°F oven so it can be cooked at the end of the evening or overnight.

5 to 10 lbs of beef roast
1 clove of garlic per lb of meat
¼ Cup of red wine
¼ Cup of Olive oil
1 sprig of rosemary per lb of meat
1 whole onion

Place sprigs of rosemary on the bottom of your crock or roasting pan, cover the roast with olive oil and place it on top of the rosemary sprigs. Add the garlic, onion and wine. If you want it quick cook uncovered for 3 hours or until the meat thermometer reaches 145°F remove and rest for 10 minutes and slice. Otherwise, cook uncovered for 2 hours, cover and cook for 5 or overnight.

Bacon Wrapped Pork Tenderloin

3 lb Pork Tenderloin
½ lb Bacon
Cotton butcher's string
Mineralized Salt & Black Pepper
¼ teaspoon of Crushed Red Pepper, up to ½ teaspoon per taste
1 Cup of Apricot Jam or (reconstituted dried Apricots to sauce)

Salt and pepper tenderloin, wrap with bacon and tie around with butcher's string then place of heavy duty foil (enough to cover the entire tenderloin. Mix crushed red pepper and apricot jam then spread over the tenderloin. Roll up foil to make a shallow pan. With oven at 650°F cook for 5 minutes or until bacon starts to brown and then turn over and cook for another 5 minutes. Timing will vary depending on the thickness of the meat. Measure internal meat temperature to preferred doneness (I like mine a medium cooked) but some like pork cooked longer, if you cook it longer than the 10 minutes of searing, just unroll the foil and fold it over the tenderloin.

Salmon Fillet

1 slab of Salmon
1 Tablespoon of Olive Oil
Blackened Meat Seasoning

Tear off a wide strip of heavy duty aluminum foil, smear with olive oil, place the salmon (skin side down) on it and sprinkle with blackened meat seasoning or spices of your preference. Slightly roll up all four sides of the foil to make a shallow pan slide into the oven and cook for 10 to 15 minutes depending on temperatures – do not overcook it salmon becomes very dry.

Turkey

1 Turkey, 10 to 15 lbs or whatever size you can squeeze through your oven door.
1 Onion
3 Carrots
4 Celery Sticks
¼ Cup Olive oil
Rotisserie Seasoning and Poultry Seasoning

Clean turkey, remove kidneys and pat dry. Place onion, carrots and celery inside and coat the outside with olive oil, sprinkle with Seasonings to taste. Keep your oven at 500°F or more cook for 15 minutes (or until is browns) and turn it, cook for 15 minutes until browned then cover with foil and close the door. A 10 lb turkey may only take 1-1/2 hours and a 15 lb turkey can take about 2-1/2 hours, but use a grilling thermometer to check internal meat temperatures. Remove and let it rest 10 minutes before slicing.

Beef Wellington

4 - Beef Tenderloin, cut to 1-1/2" to 2" thickness as desired
Mineralized Salt and Pepper
Coconut or Olive Oil
4 Slices of Prosciutto
1 teaspoon of yellow mustard (not brown)
1 lb Carrots cut in 1" blocks in a covered metal pan
1 lb Mushrooms – finely chopped
½ lb Puff Pastry
1 Egg
8 oz. Beef broth
½ cup of red wine

Lightly coat flat iron skillet with oil and place four steaks on the flat iron, sprinkle with salt and pepper and then place in a hot brick oven; brown both sides until at least rare or medium-rare if you prefer. You may have to move away from the direct heat or cover with tin foil for a few minutes.

Remove the steaks from the flat iron and let them rest. Place covered carrots in the brick oven near the door, out of direct heat. Meanwhile deglaze the flat iron and simmer with the mushroom pieces until sauce is thick – you can use a food processer to speed this up, reduce to a thick purée or pate – do not cover this is better when dry and not wet.

On wax paper, lay out a slice of thin prosciutto and spread on a thin layer of the mushroom paté, brush fillets with a very thin layer of yellow mustard and place in the center of the paté, roll up each fillet and let rest.

You won't taste the mustard and now please check and/remove the carrots when they are tender.

On wax paper, cut the pastry dough into fourths and roll out the pastry dough so it is just large enough to wrap around the fillet. Seal all joints of the pastry dough with a beaten egg wash, leaving the joints on the bottom, brush all four pastries with the remaining egg wash then score the tops of each with a crisscross pattern (but don't cut through).

Place the four fillet pastries back on a flat iron and into the brick oven away from direct heat (450°F) until the pastry dough is golden brown, you may have to turn them or you can cover them with aluminum foil to ensure the meat is hot or if you prefer until the meat is at the temperature you desire. Cook at least until the pastry is medium brown.

Often beef broth and red wine are reduced with a little butter to serve with beef wellington; it goes very well with the pastry. This step can be done much earlier or the day prior.

Brick Oven Apple Pie:

Pastry Ingredients
½ stick of butter
1 cup of all-purpose flour
½ teaspoon of salt
½ Tablespoon of ice water

Mix the first three ingredients above and sprinkle in water enough to allow the dough to stay formed and then refrigerate, while completing the rest.

2 Apples, peeled, cored and thinly sliced.
¼ Teaspoon of Cinnamon mixed
1 Tablespoon of raw sugar.

Roll out dough, place on flat iron and roll up edges. Sprinkle half the cinnamon/sugar mixture on the rolled out dough, layer the apple slices neatly around the dough, sprinkle the remainder of the cinnamon and bake in the brick oven for 10 minutes at about 500°F, until the juice thickens and bubbles.

Craving something different or a different way to prepare a dish? Millions of ideas are on the internet and many are very basic yet delivery unsurpassed flavor.

ESTIMATING MATERIALS

Material	32" by 36"	36" by 48".
Lumber	2" x 10" ~ 20ft	2" x 10" ~ 28ft
Rebar 5/8"	6 – 8ft pieces	8 – 8ft pieces
Foundation Slab	10 bags 94lb	15 bags 94lb
Block 8" x 16" (nominal height hearth)	54	90
Mortar for foundation	5 bags	
Lumber	¾" x 6" ~ 20ft	¾" x 6" ~ 22ft
Rebar 5/8"	7 – 8ft pieces	10 – 8ft pieces
Oven Base Slab #1	6 bags 94b	10 bags 94lb
Oven Base Slab #2 – Insulating Slab	6 bags 94lb	10 bags 94lb
Vermiculite for Oven Insulating Concrete	2 bags	4 bags
Refractory Mortar (fire clay)	5 – 50lb bags	8 – 50lb bags
Fire Bricks for Hearth	55	88
Fire Bricks for Oven Walls	40	64
Fire Bricks for Oven Dome	100	144
Fire Bricks for Outer Arches and Flue	48	75

Lintels (only required for flat doorways)	- ¼" x 2" x 2" x 24" -	

Reinforcing Wire 6"x6"	3 ft x 5 ft	4 ft x 6 ft
Oven Insulating Concrete	8 bags 90lb	12 bags 90lbs
Vermiculite for Oven Insulating Concrete	2 bags	4 bags

Commercial Heavy Duty Aluminum Foil	Two rolls

Chimney Flue pipe at least 8" by 8" and enough for 12 feet horizontal & vertical runs

Finish Brick & Chimney are Design Specific: 2 bundles(pallets) but up to 4

Other Materials: Heat Resistant Foam Insulation, Furnace Door gasket separating the hearth from the brick façade, OSB and/or plywood & 2" x 4" for arch forms; 1 sheet of 2" thick foam board for oven arches, Concrete Cap for chimney, left over vermiculite for insulation and high temperature glass insulation (no paper) if desired and sand to match concrete. Finally, you have to select roofing materials, I have suggested metal roofing to avoid any fire hazards and after the roof is in place it drip edges will need caulking

Made in the USA
Charleston, SC
14 March 2014